# Prince Edward Island Memories

# *Prince Edward Island Memories*

Written and Edited by Laurie Brinklow

Taste of PEI Compiled by
George Campbell and Ruth Hunter

Artwork by Hannelore Kennedy

TRAVEL MEMORIES PRESS
Indianapolis • Toronto

*Prince Edward Island Memories*
First Edition

Text © 2002 by Laurie Brinklow
Artwork © 2002 by Hannelore Kennedy

*Anne of Green Gables, Green Gables House,*
and other images of "Anne" are trademarks and Canadian official marks
of the Anne of Green Gables Licensing Authority Inc.,
used under licence by Travel Memories Press.

*"L. M. Montgomery"* is a trademark of the heirs of L. M. Montgomery Inc.

All rights reserved
ISBN 0-89730-234-6

Publisher: R. J. Berg
Series Editor: Ginny Berg

TRAVEL MEMORIES PRESS
P. O. Box 30225
Indianapolis, IN 46230-0225
Phone 800.638.3909 or 317.251.4640

Printed in Italy

*Front cover illustration: Green Gables House, Prince Edward Island National Park*
*Back cover illustration: South Shore, Prince Edward Island*

## Contents

Acknowledgements  viii

List of Illustrations  ix

"The fairest land 'tis possible to see..."  1

"Nowhere is there a spot not measured by hands..."  5

The Birthplace of Canada: Charlottetown  7

Victoria-by-the-Sea  10

Summerside  12

The Acadians  14

Lighthouses  17

"Islanders we'll always be..."  21

Of Shipbuilding and Song Making and Oyster Shucking  23

The Land of Anne  27

The Japanese Connection  31

Made in PEI  33

*". . . these are a few of my favourite things . . ."* 37

*Prince Edward Island National Park* 40

*Confederation Trail* 43

*Montague the Beautiful* 46

*Into the East* 49

*More Tastes of PEI* 53

Prince Edward Island Historical Timeline 63

Annual Festivals and Events 66

Index 67

# *Acknowledgements*

Sincere thanks go to

Harry Baglole, Institute of Island Studies, and Ed MacDonald, Department of History, both at the University of Prince Edward Island, for their knowledge of history and their willingness to share it;

Carol Horne, Department of Tourism, for what she knows about PEI, as well as whom she knows;

J. Estelle Reddin, retired Home Economics Professor, UPEI, for her extra-special attention to detail on the recipes;

the cooks, restaurant owners, and chefs who shared their marvellous recipes with us;

the computer gurus who created and maintain the award-winning Government of PEI Web site, www.gov.pe.ca, where you can find everything you need to know about the Island—and then some;

Island poet Milton Acorn for "Nowhere is there a spot not measured by hands …" from his poem "The Island";

B.C. singer/songwriter Gary Fjellgaard for "Islanders we'll always be …" from his song "Islanders"; and

Richard Rodgers and Oscar Hammerstein II for "… these are a few of my favourite things …" from their song "My Favourite Things" in *Sound of Music*.

# Illustrations

Cavendish United Church   v
Province House National Historic Site, Charlottetown   x
South Shore   4
Beaconsfield Heritage House, Charlottetown   9
West Point Lighthouse   16
Lupins   19
New London Wharf   20
Yeo House at the Green Park Shipbuilding Museum, Port Hill   25
Anne of Green Gables Museum at Silver Bush, Park Corner   29
North Rustico Scene   35
North Shore Cliffs   36
Dalvay-by-the-Sea, Prince Edward Island National Park   41
Confederation Trail   45
MV Confederation   48
Potato Fields, Stanhope   52
Elephant Rock, North Cape   61
Tignish Run Lighthouse   62
Confederation Bridge   65

# *"The fairest land 'tis possible to see..."*

The first European visitors to these shores were most likely Viking adventurers who explored the southern Gulf of St. Lawrence a thousand years ago. Coming, as they did, from glacier country in Iceland and Greenland, they were so impressed by the green bounty they found here that they called it Vinland ("wine land" or "land of grapes"). On his June 1534 voyage to the New World, French explorer Jacques Cartier called the Island "the fairest land 'tis possible to see."

Yet not everyone agreed: In the late 1820s, William Cobbett, a Member of the British Parliament, "expressed . . . a widely held British opinion" that the Island was "a rascally heap of sand, rock and swamp . . ." that . . . "bears nothing but potatoes." Today

Islanders—and even some visitors—spot the striking red cliffs bordered by blue sea and sky, and say, "This is home."

The smallest of Canada's ten provinces, Prince Edward Island measures 230 kilometres (143 miles) from tip to tip. It is nestled like a spoon close upon the coast of Nova Scotia and New Brunswick, with its South Shore separated from the mainland by the Northumberland Strait and its North Shore washed by the Gulf of St. Lawrence. The Island's aboriginal inhabitants, the Mi'kmaq, called it Abegweit, commonly translated as "cradled in the waves." In 1799 it was named for Prince Edward, duke of Kent, one of King George III's younger sons who was then commander of the British garrison in Halifax and, later, father of Queen Victoria.

At its narrowest point, the Island is 6 kilometres (not quite 4 miles) across; at its widest, 64 kilometres (about 40 miles). For most of its history, it was accessible only by boat or, during the winter months, over the ice. More recently, travellers could come by ferry, from New Brunswick to the southwest or from Nova Scotia to the southeast. In June 1997, the Island was permanently joined to the mainland by the 12.9-kilometre-long (8-mile) Confederation Bridge, a monumental construction that was not without its controversies: "If we have a bridge," people asked, "will we still be an island?"

Prince Edward Island is perhaps best known for its red soil (resulting from the oxidized iron or rust content), its potatoes (about 110,000 acres in production and over half the Island's total annual farm receipts—and for which there's even a museum, in O'Leary), its lobster (at one time used for fertilizer—and sure proof that you were poor if you took lobster sandwiches in your lunch box—and now fetching as much as $12 a pound in local grocery stores), and *Anne of Green Gables* (a fictional, spirited, red-haired orphan who has charmed generations of readers around the world).

The Island works some sort of magic, making one want to set down roots in its fertile soil and raise one's children in safety with a quality of life that is hard to find elsewhere. Often called Spud Island or the Garden of the Gulf, it is likened to a well-tended garden, with its patchwork fields of bright reds and greens against a backdrop of various shades of blue. Its sandy shores and sandstone cliffs define it, giving the Island a beginning and an end.

Island poet Milton Acorn said simply, Prince Edward Island is "the wave-lined edge of home."

# "Nowhere is there a spot not measured by hands..."

It is not known exactly when the Island's aboriginal inhabitants crossed the Strait and settled in Prince Edward Island, but historical and archaeological evidence tells us that their sophisticated society relied on the bounty of the land and the ocean to survive.

European settlers, mostly from France, began coming to Prince Edward Island in the early 1700s. They called themselves Acadians, after the name given by the French to the North American maritime territories. In 1758, following early British victories in the Seven Years War, the British expelled the Acadians, deporting about four thousand of the Island's Acadians directly to France. Some migrated to Louisiana, where they're still called Cajuns (derived from the word Acadians). Fortunately, some escaped or eventually made their way back to PEI after the war ended in 1763.

In 1764–5, British surveyor Captain Samuel Holland divided the Island into sixty-seven lots of approximately twenty thousand acres each and established three counties: Queen's, King's, and Prince. In 1767, the lots were distributed in a lottery to British noblemen, merchants, and army officers. They promised to establish their estates with immigrants who would pay them rent for the privilege of farming the land. Thus began the Land Question—years of struggle between landowners and tenants, resulting in feuds, uprisings, and generations of hardship. The leasehold system ended after Prince Edward Island joined Canada as a province in 1873, but landowners' rights are still a hot topic on the Island.

Today the pride that Islanders take in their land is evident throughout the countryside: Nowhere is there a place so well manicured as Prince Edward Island.

# The Birthplace of Canada: Charlottetown

The capital of Prince Edward Island is Charlottetown, named for Queen Charlotte, wife of King George III. Laid out on an enlightened grid system (inspired by Roman models) in the mid-1700s, the city wraps itself around Charlottetown Harbour, and is filled with numerous green spaces, majestic elms, and (mostly) tasteful architecture, including stately nineteenth-century homes. The city has been called the Cradle of Confederation and the Birthplace of Canada because the 1864 Charlottetown Conference, held in Province House, led to the creation of Canada three years later. The Confederation Centre of the Arts was built next door to Province House in 1964 to commemorate the Fathers of Confederation. The lovely historic house called Beaconsfield, overlooking the harbour, is home to the PEI Museum and Heritage Foundation, which oversees the Island's extensive museum system.

# Maple-Roasted Pork Tenderloin with Fruit Confit

*L*ocated on a quiet residential street in Charlottetown is the Dundee Arms Inn—a gracious three-storey inn, complete with a pub, a well-shaded deck set amongst the maples, and an elegant dining room. When preparing this recipe, the Dundee's savvy chef makes the confit while the pork is roasting.

PREHEAT OVEN TO 350°F.

TO PREPARE MARINADE: In a small bowl, combine mustard, syrup, pepper, and salt; mix well. Place pork tenderloin in a baking pan and brush marinade on all surfaces of meat. Pour any excess marinade over tenderloin. Roast at 350°F for about 20 to 25 minutes for medium doneness. Before serving, cut pork into medallions (bite-size pieces).

TO PREPARE FRUIT CONFIT: Place clarified butter in a large sauté pan over medium heat. Add peach, pear, and plum; sauté, stirring occasionally, for 4 to 5 minutes. Add vinegar, mustard, cumin seed, and pepper; cook for 2 to 3 minutes. Add syrup and cook 2 to 3 minutes longer. Add brown sugar and cook about 1 more minute. Season with salt.

To serve, place a spoonful of confit liquid on serving plates, then top with equal portions of pork medallions. Spoon confit over and around medallions.

*Yield: 4 servings*

## Marinade

2 to 3 tablespoons Pommery mustard or other coarse-grained mustard

2 tablespoons maple syrup

1½ teaspoons cracked black pepper

½ teaspoon salt

1 pork tenderloin (about 1½ pounds), trimmed

## Fruit Confit

3 tablespoons clarified butter

1 small fresh peach, peeled and diced (about ⅓ cup)

1 small fresh pear, peeled and diced (about ⅓ cup)

1 small fresh plum, peeled and diced (about ⅓ cup)

¼ cup white vinegar

2 to 3 tablespoons Pommery mustard or other coarse-grained mustard

1 tablespoon cumin seed

1½ teaspoons cracked black pepper

2 tablespoons maple syrup

3 tablespoons brown sugar

½ teaspoon salt or to taste

# Victoria-by-the-Sea

The small South Shore village of Victoria-by-the-Sea is a favourite with visitors and locals alike. Once the Island's fourth busiest seaport, Victoria still bustles, particularly in the summertime. Well known for its theatre, artists, and artisans, this is the perfect place for an afternoon stroll to check out the art galleries and craft shops, Island Chocolates and the used-book store, and cream tea at the Orient Hotel. Stick around for dinner, then a concert or some repertory theatre at the beautifully restored Victoria Playhouse. The wharf in Victoria is lively, too, with fishing boats coming and going. On a hot summer's day, when the tide is right, you'll see kids jumping off the wharf for a cool dip.

# Seawinds Seafood Casserole

½ cup butter, divided
2 to 3 cups chopped celery
2 cups chopped onions
¾ cup flour
4½ cups milk, divided
1 pound processed cheese slices
1 pound fresh scallops
12 ounces fresh lobster, cut into bite-size pieces
12 ounces fresh shrimp, peeled and deveined
8 ounces fresh crabmeat, flaked and cartilage removed
1 teaspoon salt
¼ teaspoon pepper
Lemon slices and fresh parsley, for garnish

At the end of the wharf in Victoria-by-the-Sea, Seawinds Steak and Seafood Restaurant provides a fabulous view of the Northumberland Strait, as well as tasty chowders, mussels, and other mouth-watering dishes made from seafood purchased on the wharf. Four types of fresh seafood are featured in this delectable casserole.

PREHEAT OVEN TO 325°F. Grease a three-quart casserole; set aside.

Melt 3 tablespoons butter in a large saucepan over low heat. Add celery and onions; sauté for 3 to 5 minutes, stirring occasionally. In a small bowl, blend flour with enough cold milk (½ to ¾ cup) to make a smooth, thin paste. Add flour-milk mixture to skillet and cook, stirring constantly, for about 5 minutes or until mixture bubbles and thickens. Add remaining butter and milk along with cheese; cook over low heat for about 10 minutes or until cheese melts and sauce is thick. Watch carefully so mixture doesn't scorch. Add scallops, lobster, shrimp, and crabmeat; mix gently. Season with salt and pepper. Transfer mixture to prepared casserole and bake at 325°F for about 20 minutes or until top is golden brown. Serve with a garnish of lemon slices and parsley.

*Yield: 12 servings*

# Summerside

Summerside is the Island's second largest city. In the mid-1800s, it was a major shipbuilding centre and seaport. Today, with its natural harbour on Bedeque Bay, it continues to serve as a primary port for exporting world-famous PEI potatoes. In the early 1900s, Summerside became the world centre of an international fashion fad that showcased the locally bred silver fox. Evidence of the wealth generated by this industry is found at the International Fox Museum and Hall of Fame, and in several of the beautiful "fox houses" that still grace the city's tree-lined streets. Summerside's College of Piping is also gaining an international reputation for its world-class instruction in the Celtic performing arts such as piping, dancing, and drumming.

# Coquilles St. Jacques

When the United Empire Loyalists emigrated from the United States following the American Revolution, Summerside was one of the locations where they settled in Canada. Today, just across the street from the Harbourfront Jubilee Theatre and Eptek National Exhibition Centre, the Loyalist Country Inn serves this classic dish.

BOIL AND WHIP POTATOES. Set aside and keep warm.

TO PREPARE WHITE SAUCE: Melt butter in a small saucepan over medium heat. Add flour and whisk to mix; cook, whisking constantly, for 2 to 3 minutes or until mixture bubbles. Add milk and cook, whisking constantly, for about 5 minutes or until mixture thickens. Remove from heat and keep warm.

TO PREPARE SCALLOPS AND SAUCE: Melt 2 tablespoons butter in a large skillet over medium heat. Add scallops and sauté for about 2 minutes. Add lemon juice, then transfer scallops and juice to a bowl. Melt remaining butter in the same skillet. Add mushrooms and green onions; sauté for 2 minutes. Add wine and liquid from scallops. Bring to a boil and cook until mixture is reduced by one-third. Add white sauce and mix well. Season with salt and pepper.

Preheat oven to broil. Place scallops in four individual baking dishes or a shallow casserole. Pour sauce over scallops, then pipe or spoon potatoes around the edges. Sprinkle with cheese. Broil four inches from heat source for about 3 to 5 minutes or until bubbly and slightly browned. Watch closely so tops don't burn. Serve with a garnish of lemon wedges and parsley sprigs.

*Yield: 4 to 6 servings*

---

4 medium potatoes

### White Sauce
2 tablespoons butter
2 tablespoons flour
1 cup milk

### Scallops and Sauce
4 tablespoons butter, divided
1½ pounds fresh scallops
2 tablespoons lemon juice
6 medium mushrooms, sliced
2 green onions, sliced
½ cup white wine
1 cup white sauce
Salt and pepper
½ cup grated mozzarella cheese
Lemon wedges and parsley sprigs, for garnish

# The Acadians

Nearly one-quarter of the Island's ancestry can be traced to Acadie, the area centred around the Bay of Fundy where French settlers farmed as early as the 1600s. Acadian traditions and culture are strong and vibrant in villages such as Abram-Village, Wellington, Mont-Carmel, Tignish, and Rustico, where residents proudly fly the Acadian flag of red, white, and blue with a yellow star. The Acadian Museum in Miscouche and the Farmers' Bank in South Rustico chronicle the Acadians' many contributions to the Island; the Festival Acadien is held every summer in Évangéline; and internationally known singers and musicians, such as Angèle Arsenault and Lennie Gallant, and the group Barachois, can be heard on the Island throughout the year.

# Pâté (Meat Pie)

Mémé Jane's Restaurant—located in Miscouche, in the heart of Acadian country—specializes in traditional French Acadian dishes. Pâté is typically served at Christmastime, when the family gets together for a "lunch" following Midnight Mass.

TO PREPARE FILLING: In a large pot, combine pork, chicken, onions, pickling spices, and 3 tablespoons summer savory; add enough water to cover. Bring to a boil, then reduce heat and simmer for at least 30 minutes or until meat is tender. Drain meat, reserving broth. Set meat aside to cool. Strain broth and discard pickling spices. Debone meat and cut into chunks. Season with summer savory, coriander, salt, and pepper; mix well.

TO PREPARE PASTRY: In a large mixing bowl, combine flour, baking powder, and salt. Using a pastry blender, cut in shortening until mixture resembles coarse crumbs. Break egg into a one-cup measure and beat lightly. Add vinegar and enough water to fill the cup. Pour liquid into flour mixture and mix until a soft dough forms. Divide dough into eight equal portions. On a floured surface, roll out four portions of dough so each will fit an eight-inch pie plate. Line four pie plates with pastry. Roll out remaining four portions of dough to use as top crusts.

TO PREPARE PÂTÉ: Preheat oven to 375ºF. Divide filling equally among the four pastry-lined pie plates. Drizzle some of the reserved broth over filling to moisten. Place top crusts over filling, then pinch edges of pastry to seal. Cut slits in top crusts so steam can escape. Bake at 375ºF for 1 hour or until lightly browned.

*Yield: 4 pies, 6 servings each*

## Filling

4 pounds fresh pork shoulder or butt, whole or cut into pieces

4 pounds chicken, cut into pieces

4 large onions, chopped

3 tablespoons pickling spices, tied in a cheesecloth bag

3 tablespoons summer savory

Summer savory, crushed coriander, salt, and pepper (to taste)

## Pastry

5 cups white flour

1 teaspoon baking powder

1 teaspoon salt

1 pound (2½ cups) vegetable shortening

1 egg

1 tablespoon vinegar

# Lighthouses

Prince Edward Island has had its fair share of shipwrecks and sea disasters, but encircling the Island's shores are those enduring symbols of protection and beacons of hope: lighthouses. The oldest was built in Point Prim in 1846. Just over 18 metres (60 feet) high, it is visible from the Charlottetown waterfront. West Point Lighthouse, 20.7 metres (about 68 feet) high, was built in 1875 near the Island's westernmost edge, looking out over the Northumberland Strait to New Brunswick. Today an automated lighthouse, the light was operated manually until 1963. Restored in 1984, the lighthouse now houses a museum that documents the history of the Island's lighthouses. Guest rooms were also added, making West Point the first inn in Canada situated in a working lighthouse.

# Butterscotch Pie

The West Point Lighthouse is a proud participant in the Prince Edward Island Lighthouse Society's Follow the Lights program. Plaques have been placed on the Island's most prominent lighthouses, and if you visit at least eight and make rubbings of the nameplates, you can receive a Commemorative PEI Lighthouses Certificate. Visitors to the West Point Lighthouse Restaurant can also sample this delicious pie.

TO PREPARE FILLING: Combine brown sugar and flour in a small bowl; stir to mix. In a separate microwave-safe bowl, combine milk and egg yolks; whisk to mix. Add brown sugar mixture and salt to milk mixture; mix well. Microwave on High for 60 seconds, then whisk. Continue microwaving on High, whisking every 40 seconds, until mixture reaches desired thickness. Add butter and vanilla; mix well. Cool slightly, then pour into baked pie crust.

TO PREPARE MERINGUE: Preheat oven to 350°F. Beat egg whites until foamy. Gradually add sugar, beating until whites stand in soft peaks. Spread meringue evenly over pie, sealing edges. Bake at 350°F for about 5 minutes or until meringue is lightly browned.

*Yield: 6 to 8 servings*

## Filling

1 cup brown sugar
⅓ cup flour
2 cups milk
2 egg yolks
¼ teaspoon salt
1 teaspoon butter
1 teaspoon vanilla

1 baked pie crust

## Meringue

2 egg whites
¼ cup white sugar

## *"Islanders we'll always be..."*

Prince Edward Island is home to 139,000 people of mainly English, French, Scots, and Irish descent—with a smattering of other nationalities such as Dutch and Lebanese—as well as the Mi'kmaq, many of whom live on land set aside for them in Lennox Island, Rocky Point, and Scotchfort. Islanders farm, and they fish, and they process what they harvest. They work for government and they run businesses. They compete in the knowledge economy and information technology sectors. And they work in tourism, which vies with agriculture for top billing as the Island's number-one industry.

But the question "Who is an Islander?" is always good for a few hours of raucous debate. Some say you have to be born and bred seven generations to be an Islander, while others say you must be conceived above the high-water mark. CFAs (Come From Aways) often call themselves born-again Islanders, realizing that being born here is the strongest currency.

Perhaps it's the shared history and determination left over from struggles about the Land Question that make Islanders so fiercely proud to live here. Perhaps it's the independence that comes from living on an Island, where you know you're set apart from the mainland and you have to stick together as a community in order to thrive. Perhaps it's sheer stubbornness, being born of a small place and wanting to remain independent in a quickly homogenizing world.

There's something very special about being part of the tight, interlocking mosaic that is Prince Edward Island. It can make some people feel hemmed in, but for others, there's a measure of comfort in knowing exactly what your boundaries are.

## Of Shipbuilding and Song Making and Oyster Shucking

The area around the village of Tyne Valley was a thriving shipbuilding community in the 1800s. The historic Yeo House and Green Park Shipbuilding Museum take us back to the days when building ships and sailing them around the world were the mainstays of the Island's economy. Tyne Valley was also the birthplace of Larry Gorman, one of the Island's most notorious satirical "song makers." If Larry didn't like someone, he would "song" them! Britannia Hall hosts an annual folk festival bearing Gorman's name, where Island singers and songwriters perform. And because of its location near Malpeque Bay, a rich oyster-harvesting area, Tyne Valley is also known for Malpeque oysters, ranked among the world's finest. The oyster is celebrated at the annual Tyne Valley Oyster Festival.

# Shipwright's Oysters

Malpeque oysters, lobster, and shellfish—fresh from the sea. PEI potatoes, organic fruits, and vegetables—fresh from the land. This bountiful Island harvest is reflected in the dishes featured on chef Calvin Burt's menu of regional cookery at the Shipwright's Café, which is situated in an 1880s farmhouse in Margate.

PREHEAT OVEN TO BROIL.

Wash and shuck oysters, then place in a baking pan along with their liquor (juice). Arrange spinach leaves over oysters, then top with cheeses. Place on top rack of oven and broil for 5 to 10 minutes or until cheese melts and turns light brown.

To serve, sprinkle parsley or herbs on serving plates. Spoon oysters, spinach, and cheese on top of herbs. Garnish with lemon wedges and serve with garlic toast.

*24 Malpeque oysters (6 per serving)*

*1 bunch fresh spinach (about 12 ounces)*

*3 ounces medium cheddar cheese, grated (about ¾ cup)*

*3 ounces mozzarella cheese, grated (about ¾ cup)*

*½ cup (approximately) chopped fresh parsley or your favourite fresh herbs*

*Lemon wedges (for garnish)*

*Garlic toast*

*Yield: 4 servings*

H. kennedy

# Fresh Atlantic Salmon en Papillote

*6 tablespoons vegetable oil*
*1 large stalk celery, finely diced*
*½ onion, finely diced*
*8 ounces mushrooms, sliced*
*Salt and pepper*
*6 fresh Atlantic salmon fillets or steaks (5 to 6 ounces each)*
*6 pieces 10-inch-square parchment paper*

This dish is one of the Shipwright's most requested presentations of salmon. Fresh from the ice-cold Atlantic, the firm-fleshed fish is a joy to prepare and serve. Expect rave reviews when the paper envelopes are opened right at the table, releasing the wonderful aromas of salmon and vegetables.

PREHEAT OVEN TO 350°F.

Heat oil in a frying pan. Add celery, onion, and mushrooms; sauté for 3 to 5 minutes, stirring occasionally. Season with salt and pepper. Place one piece of salmon off-center on a square of parchment paper and top with one-sixth of the vegetable mixture. Fold parchment over salmon and vegetables, then crimp edges of paper together tightly to form an envelope. Repeat with remaining salmon and vegetables. Place parchment envelopes on a sturdy baking sheet and bake at 350°F for 20 to 30 minutes.

To serve, place envelopes on dinner plates and cut a slit in the top of each envelope at the table.

*Yield: 6 servings*

# The Land Of *Anne*

Nearly a million visitors come to the Island each year. They come for the beautiful scenery and the beaches. They come to slow down, to experience a working rural landscape reminiscent of a simpler time. And they come to see the land that Lucy Maud Montgomery wrote about. L. M. Montgomery was born in 1874 in Clifton (now New London) and raised in Cavendish by her maternal grandparents. Her most famous novel, *Anne of Green Gables,* features the beloved red-headed heroine, Anne Shirley, revered for her spunk and love of life. Anne's love of words led her to give special names to her favourite places, from Lover's Lane and the White Way of Delight to the Haunted Wood and the Lake of Shining Waters.

# Nutmeg Scones

In her journals, L. M. Montgomery wrote about visiting her Campbell cousins at their home, which she called Silver Bush. Today the Campbells' house is the Anne of Green Gables Museum, and the adjacent Shining Waters Tea Room, owned by George and Maureen Campbell, offers a warm welcome and a refreshing snack.

PREHEAT OVEN TO 425°F.

Break eggs into a mixing bowl and beat by hand. Add margarine or butter and shortening; beat until thoroughly creamed. Combine flour, brown sugar, cream of tartar, soda, salt, and nutmeg. Add raisins or mixed dried fruit to dry ingredients and mix well. Add dry ingredients to creamed mixture alternately with milk, stirring to form a soft dough. (If dough is too moist, add a bit more flour.) Turn out onto a floured surface and divide dough into three equal portions. Roll out one portion or pat by hand to form a circle ½-inch thick. Cut circle like a pie into twelve wedges, then brush with egg white. Place wedges on an ungreased baking sheet. Repeat with remaining portions of dough. Bake at 425°F for 12 to 15 minutes. Serve warm with butter.

*2 eggs*
*½ cup margarine or butter, softened*
*½ cup vegetable shortening*
*6 cups flour*
*1½ cups brown sugar*
*4 teaspoons cream of tartar*
*2 teaspoons baking soda*
*2 teaspoons salt*
*1 teaspoon nutmeg*
*1 cup raisins or mixed dried fruit*
*1½ cups milk*
*Egg white, slightly beaten*
*(to brush on unbaked scones)*

*Yield: 36 scones*

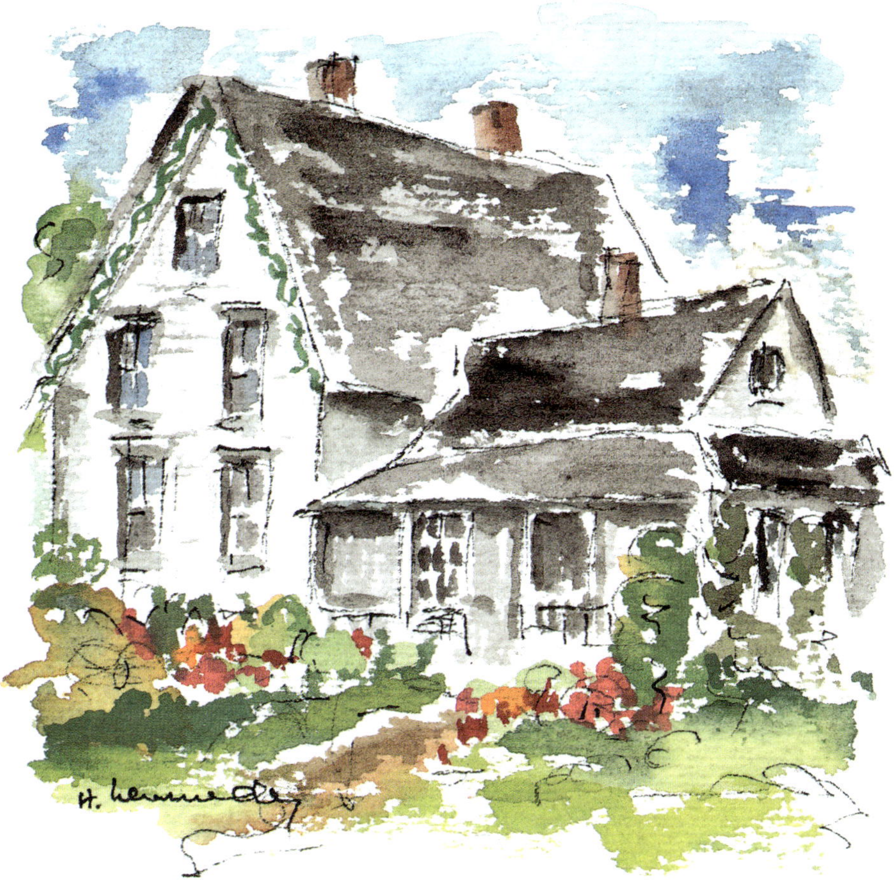

# Icebox Ginger Cookies

*Lucy Maud Montgomery described her aunt and uncle's home as "a big white beautiful house smothered in orchards that was the wonder castle of my childhood." After a carriage ride along the Lake of Shining Waters, visitors today can snack on a ginger cookie at the Shining Waters Tea Room.*

*1 cup vegetable shortening*
*⅔ cup molasses*
*⅓ cup brown sugar*
*3 cups flour*
*2 teaspoons baking soda*
*2 teaspoons powdered ginger*
*1 teaspoon cinnamon*
*1 teaspoon salt*

IN A MIXING BOWL, combine shortening, molasses, and brown sugar; beat until thoroughly creamed. Sift together flour, soda, ginger, cinnamon, and salt. Add dry ingredients to creamed mixture and mix well. Form dough into a roll about two inches in diameter. Wrap dough in waxed paper and refrigerate for at least 1 hour.

When ready to bake, preheat oven to 350°F. Remove waxed paper and cut dough into ¼-inch slices. Place on an ungreased baking sheet and bake at 350°F for 10 to 15 minutes.

*Yield: 48 cookies*

# The Japanese Connection

Anne Shirley's spirited nature has made her a role model for young girls around the world—and nowhere more so than in Japan, where she is known as Akage no An ("red-haired Anne"). In the 1950s, L. M. Montgomery's novel was translated into Japanese and incorporated into the school curriculum. Japanese readers of all ages eagerly embraced Anne's optimism and imagination, and over the years, Prince Edward Island has become a mecca for thousands of Japanese tourists who make the pilgrimage to the home of their fictional heroine. Many young Japanese couples even have their weddings here. Two villages along the North Shore are favourite destinations: Cavendish, with its historic Green Gables House, and New London, featuring Montgomery's birthplace.

# New Moon Pudding

*1 lemon*

*4 cups milk*

*6 eggs, separated*

*1 cup sugar, divided*

*2 cups soft bread crumbs (best made with homemade white bread)*

*Whipped cream flavoured with icing sugar and Cointreau*

Terry Kamikawa's passion for Anne led her to research and publish a cookbook and history of Island life for Japanese readers. She found the recipe for New Moon Pudding in L. M. Montgomery's Selected Journals, *and now serves the lemony treat at the Blue Winds Tea Room in the refurbished parlour of her New London farmhouse.*

PREHEAT OVEN TO 375ºF. Grease a 10x2½-inch round baking dish; set aside.

Grate rind from lemon, then squeeze juice (set juice aside for later use). In a large mixing bowl, combine lemon rind, milk, slightly beaten egg yolks, and ⅔ cup sugar; mix well. Add bread crumbs and stir gently until well blended. Pour into prepared baking dish, then set dish in a larger, sturdy baking pan. Pour hot water into the baking pan to a depth of one inch, creating a water bath. Carefully place pan in oven and bake at 375ºF for 40 to 50 minutes or until a knife inserted about one inch from the edge comes out clean.

When pudding is nearly done, beat egg whites with remaining ⅓ cup sugar until whites stand in soft peaks. Gradually stir in lemon juice. When pudding is done, remove dish from oven and spread meringue evenly over top, sealing edges. Increase oven temperature to broil. Return dish to oven for about 2 minutes or until meringue is browned. Watch closely so the meringue doesn't burn. Remove from oven and cool. Serve with flavoured whipped cream.

*Yield: 10 to 12 servings*

# Made in PEI

Prince Edward Island's rich cultural heritage is played out time and time again by the proliferation of artistic festivals, theatre offerings, paintings, crafts, books, and music that are produced here every year. Many Canadians remember "Don Messer and His Islanders," a CBC-TV program that featured traditional Down East fiddling and Maritime music, leaving a legacy that continues today. Amateur theatre abounds in many of the Island's smaller communities, and wonderful crafts—pottery, weaving, woodwork, glasswork, quilts—are created on the Island by some of the country's finest artists and artisans. Many, choosing the Island as their muse, settled here during the back-to-the-land movement of the 1970s. Others were born here and continue the traditions of the past.

# Salmon Pie

The Prince Edward Island Preserve Company had its humble beginnings in a borrowed kitchen, but the first preserve Bruce MacNaughton produced was anything but humble: Strawberry and Grand Marnier. Today a renovated 1913 butter factory in New Glasgow is where he sells his preserves and serves meals such as this delectable Salmon Pie in a café overlooking the River Clyde.

PREHEAT OVEN TO 350°F.

Place all ingredients (except pastry) in a food processor and process until mixture is well blended. Pour filling into unbaked pastry shell. Cover with top crust, then pinch edges of pastry to seal. Cut slits in top crust. Bake at 350°F for 40 minutes. Remove from oven and cool 5 minutes before serving.

SERVING NOTE: Serve with a side salad for a light meal.

---

12 ounces raw or cooked salmon
8 ounces cream cheese, cubed
3 eggs
¾ cup heavy cream
2 tablespoons white wine
2 tablespoons snipped chives
1 teaspoon onion powder
½ teaspoon dried tarragon
Salt and pepper
Pastry for a two-crust pie

*Yield: 6 servings*

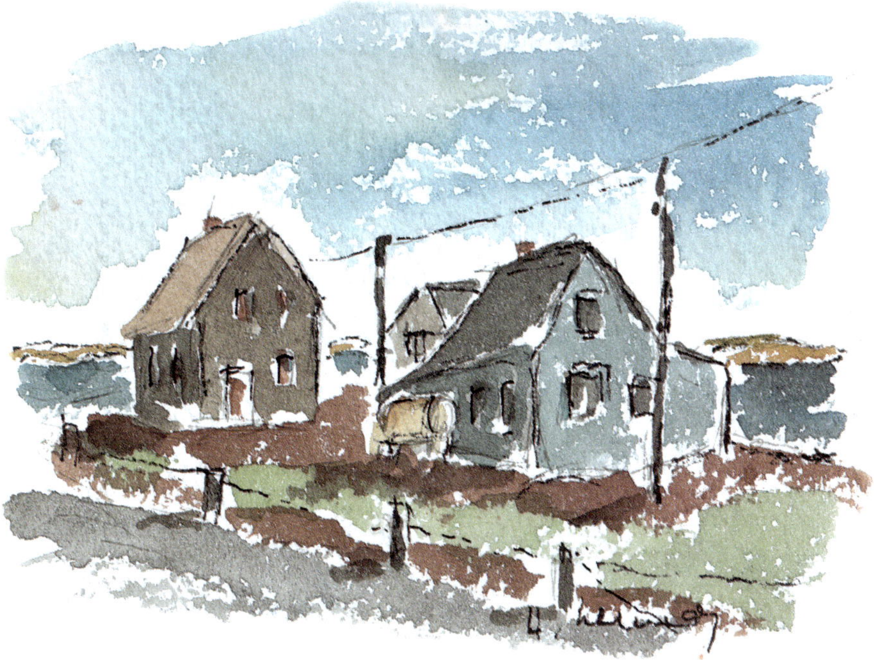

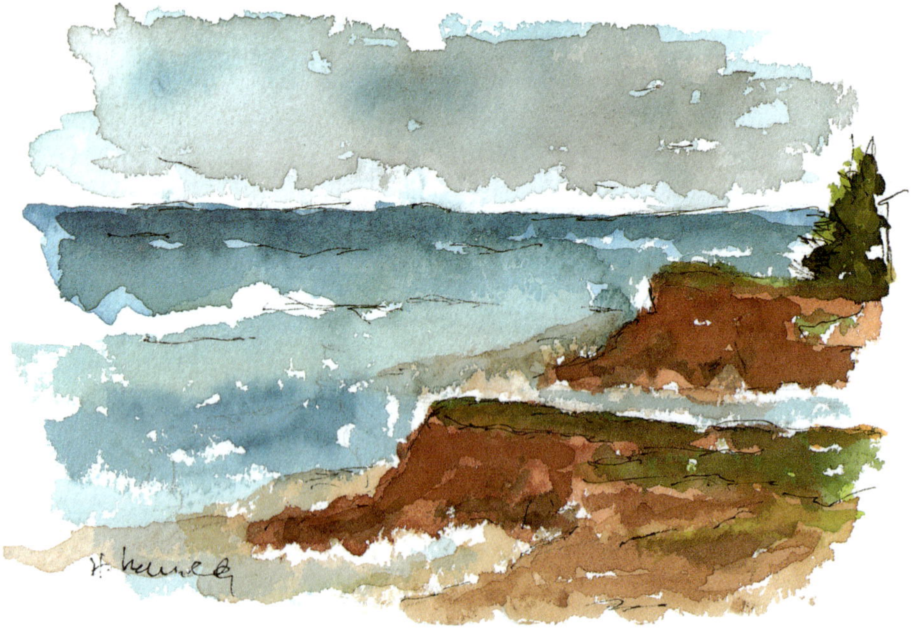

*"... these are a few of my favourite things ..."*

For some in Prince Edward Island, the year begins in autumn, when the colours start to change and the nesting instinct sets in. The Storytelling Festival gets us in the mood for tucking in, for swapping stories and sharing music. Weekend mornings in September and October are perfect times for walks with friends, checking out the myriad walking trails that crisscross the Island. The boardwalk at the national park at Greenwich—through the marsh down to a pristine beach—makes a rare dune system accessible without endangering a sensitive ecosystem. The trails at Macphail Homestead at Orwell and at Strathgartney Provincial Park in the Bonshaw Hills are favourites, as are the Bubbling Springs and Farmlands Trail in the national park near Dalvay and the Homestead Trail in Cavendish. The Confederation Trail, the Island leg of the TransCanada Trail of abandoned railway lines that have been resurfaced, makes it possible to bicycle or walk from nearly one end of the Island to the other.

In winter, when snow hangs heavy in the trees and the sun trickles weakly through the branches, some of these trails are open for cross-country skiing. Skating on Dalvay Pond or—believe it or not—walks on the beach, clambering over ice pans strewn haphazardly across the sand, are brisk and life-affirming, especially with a mug of hot chocolate waiting at the other end. "Storm days," when a snowstorm shuts down the Island, are devoutly wished for by children—and sometimes their parents too. And the Charlottetown Farmers' Market on Saturday mornings—with organic produce, crafts, fresh baked goods, and ethnic food—is a tradition the entire year. It has been dubbed a revolving party, a warm and bright spot especially welcome during those dark winter days.

Spring is usually a painfully drawn-out affair, preceded by "mud season," when secondary roads and unpaved driveways become bogs of squishy red goop. But when those fragrant springtime breezes begin to stir new leaves and hearts, you know winter's end is in sight. Soon tractors will be out on the land, drawing lines in red fields, getting ready for new planting, clouds of seagulls in tow. Long V's of Canada geese will sketch their matching lines across the sky, and Islanders will be painting their fences and planting their flowers, happy to be outdoors once more.

Summer is that blissfully lazy time when anything's possible: sleepy days on a favourite North Shore beach, lolling about in the warmest coastal waters north of the Carolinas, or sailing across Charlottetown Harbour to Holland Cove with friends. Sitting under an umbrella sipping a latté or an Italian soda, listening to music or just watching the world go by on Charlottetown's Victoria Row. Going for a drive along the Northumberland Strait, stopping at Rossignol Winery in Little Sands for a sample, or heading over to North Rustico to catch a sunset at Orby Head. Or dinner and a concert at the Trailside Café in Mount Stewart, a play in Victoria, a ceilidh in Monticello or at the Orwell Corner Historic Village, or the Larry Gorman Festival in Tyne Valley.

Do you see now why we stay?

# Prince Edward Island National Park

Curving along the Island's North Shore is Prince Edward Island National Park, Canada's smallest national park at only 27 square kilometres (about 10½ square miles). Two of the Island's most visited cultural landmarks—Green Gables House and Dalvay-by-the-Sea—are located within the park's boundaries. The park also protects some of the world's most spectacular and fragile dune systems while at the same time offering itself as a summer playground to thousands of tourists every year. Miles of sandy beaches are the park's main attraction, but interpretive walks, campgrounds, and natural woodlands and marshes allow you to feel like you're getting away from it all—something that is easy to do in Prince Edward Island.

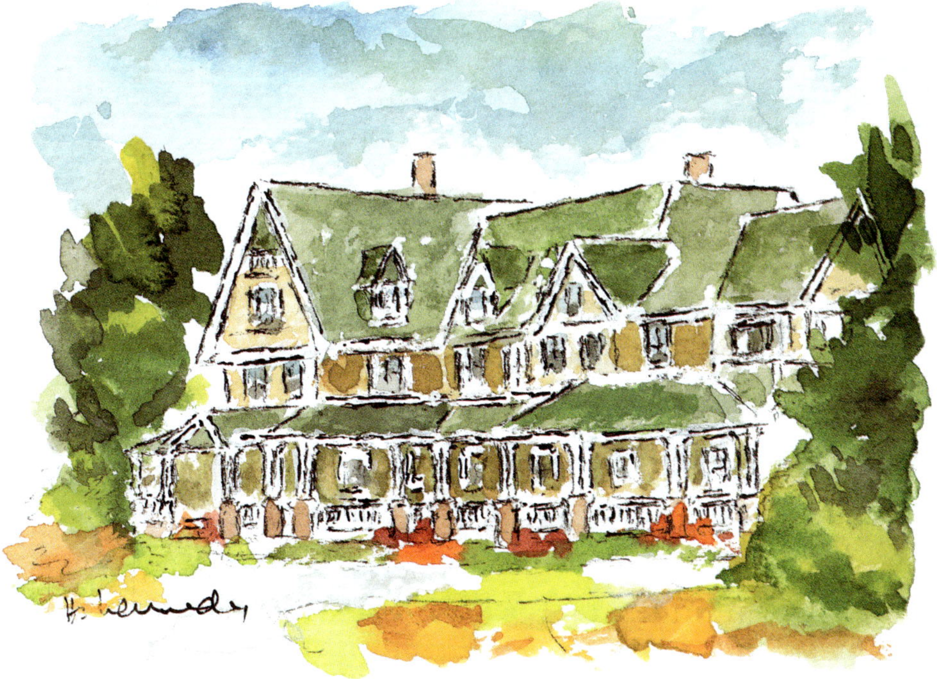

# Sticky Date Pudding with Toffee Sauce

D*alvay-by-the-Sea is a gracious inn with spacious lawns and a lovely lake. Dalvay was built in 1896 as a summer home for Standard Oil president Alexander MacDonald, who named it for his ancestral home in Scotland. The inn was seen as the White Sands Hotel in the screen version of* Anne of Green Gables. *This is one of Dalvay's most requested desserts.*

COMBINE WATER AND DATES in a saucepan and bring to a boil. Boil for 2 minutes. Add soda and stir to mix. Remove from heat and let sit for 30 minutes. Line an 8x8-inch cake pan with waxed paper; set aside. Preheat oven to 375°F.

TO PREPARE PUDDING: Cream sugar and butter in a mixing bowl. Add eggs, one at a time, mixing well after each addition. Sift together flour, baking powder, and ginger. Fold dry ingredients into creamed mixture. Add dates (do not drain) and mix well. Spread batter in prepared pan, then set pan in a larger, sturdy baking pan. Pour hot water into the larger pan to a depth of about one inch, creating a water bath. Carefully place pan in oven and bake at 375°F for 30 to 35 minutes.

TO PREPARE TOFFEE SAUCE: Melt butter in a saucepan over medium heat. Add brown sugar and cook, stirring constantly, until sugar dissolves. Add cream and bring to a boil. Boil for 2 minutes. Watch closely so sauce doesn't burn. Serve pudding warm with toffee sauce and vanilla ice cream, if desired.

*Yield: 8 to 12 servings*

## Pudding

2 cups water
8 ounces dates, chopped
1½ teaspoons baking soda
1¼ cups granulated sugar
6 tablespoons butter
3 eggs
1 cup flour
1 tablespoon baking powder
½ teaspoon powdered ginger

## Toffee Sauce

⅝ cup (10 tablespoons) butter
¾ cup brown sugar
¾ cup cream

*Vanilla ice cream, if desired*

# Confederation Trail

A railway was built on the Island in 1871, but the debt quickly became too much for the tiny island colony, so paying off the railway became part of the negotiations when PEI joined Confederation in 1873. Then when trucks became more popular than trains for hauling goods, the last train disappeared from the Island landscape (in 1989), leaving behind miles of abandoned tracks. Island Trails seized the opportunity and had the railway lines resurfaced. Today the Confederation Trail winds through some of the most picturesque parts of the Island—over rolling hills, along riverbanks, across bridges, and even beside the coast—with a few branch lines to some out-of-the-way communities. The trail's gentle grade is perfect for touring.

# Oyster Stew

The Trailside Café and Inn is just a stone's throw from the Confederation Trail in Mount Stewart, at the head of the Hillsborough River. Located in an old co-op store, the café rents bicycles for a ride along the trail, and it serves up a bite to eat (such as this Oyster Stew) and sometimes live music for soothing those sore muscles.

BOIL POTATOES for about 10 minutes or just until done; drain and set aside. Melt butter in a large saucepan. Add onion and garlic; sauté over low heat, stirring occasionally, for at least 5 minutes. Place oysters and their liquor in another saucepan and cook gently over medium heat for 1 to 2 minutes, just long enough to firm the oysters. Add potatoes and oysters (with their liquor) to onion-garlic mixture; mix well. Add milk, cream, parsley, tarragon, salt, black pepper, and cayenne pepper; stir to mix. Cook over low heat just until heated through. Do not boil.

4 medium potatoes, cubed
¼ cup butter
1 onion, chopped
2 cloves garlic, chopped
24 oysters, washed and shucked (reserve liquor)
1 litre (about 4½ cups) milk
1 cup cream
3 tablespoons dried parsley
1 tablespoon dried tarragon
1 tablespoon salt
1 teaspoon black pepper
Pinch of cayenne pepper

*Yield: 6 to 8 servings*

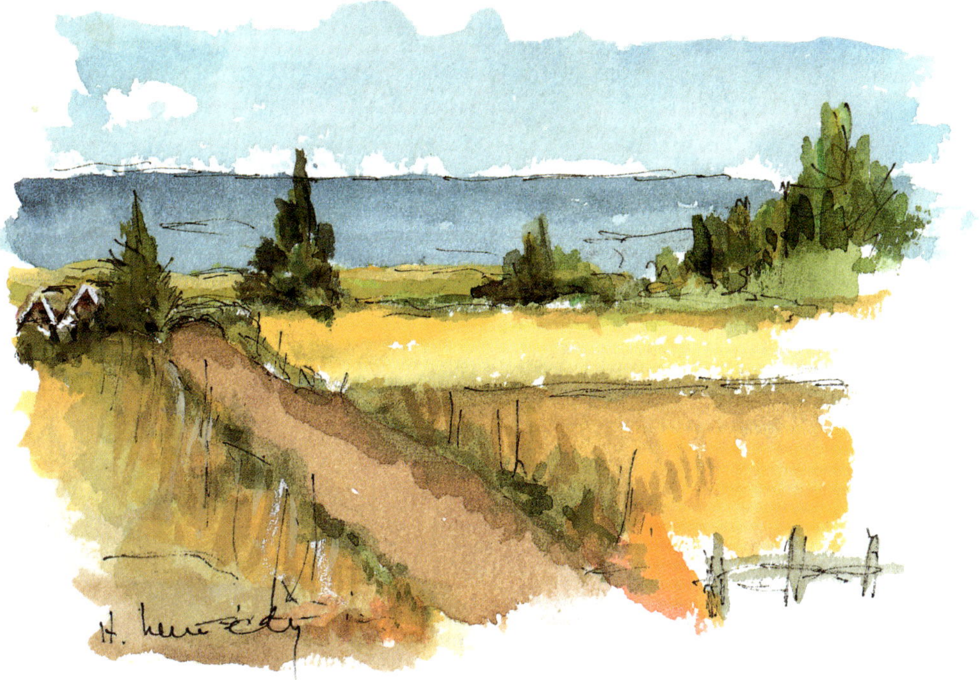

# Montague the Beautiful

The Island is rich in community. From farming towns and fishing villages to the larger urban centres, people rely on one another. It's part of the Island way of life. Montague the Beautiful is one such place, a bustling town in the Island's southeastern region. Situated on the historic Montague River, just upriver from the shipbuilding town of Georgetown, Montague is an ideal launching place for daytrips—exploring the coastal waters on a seal-watching tour, kayaking, or biking or walking on the Confederation Trail. The Garden of the Gulf Museum is a great place to while away a few hours, and golfers take note: The world-class, thirty-six-hole Dundarave and Brudenell Golf Resort is only minutes away.

# Creamy Carrot and Zucchini Soup

> 4 carrots, cut into chunks
> 2 small zucchini, cut into chunks
> 1 stalk celery, coarsely chopped
> 1 Spanish onion, coarsely chopped
> 1 apple, peeled, cored, and cut into chunks
> 2 tablespoons chicken bouillon granules
> 2 teaspoons curry powder
> ½ cup butter
> ½ cup flour
> 3 cups light cream
> Salt and pepper
> Dairy sour cream (for garnish)
> Fresh parsley or cilantro leaves, chopped (for garnish)

Overlooking the Montague River and a busy marina full of fishing boats and pleasure craft, Windows on the Water Café in Montague offers casual dining outdoors on a wraparound deck or indoors in the quaint dining room filled with antiques and atmosphere. Whenever possible, chefs use locally grown produce to create dishes such as this creamy soup.

IN A SOUP POT, combine carrots, zucchini, celery, onion, and apple. Add enough water to cover. Dissolve bouillon granules in a small amount of hot water, then add to pot along with curry powder. Bring to a boil, then reduce heat and cook for about 30 minutes or until vegetables are tender. Drain, then purée. Return vegetable purée to soup pot.

Melt butter in a saucepan. Add flour and cook over medium heat, stirring constantly, until mixture bubbles and thickens, making a roux. Add roux to vegetable purée and blend well. Cook over medium heat until mixture thickens. Add cream, salt, and pepper; mix well. Cook over low heat just until heated through. Ladle into bowls and garnish with a dollop of sour cream and a sprinkle of parsley or cilantro.

*Yield: 6 servings*

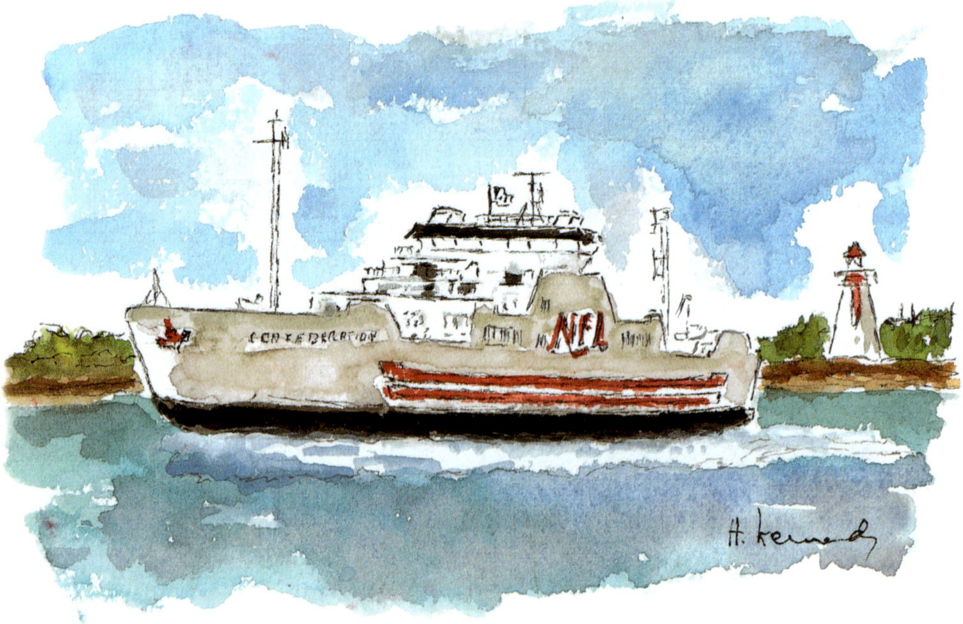
CONFEDERATION
NFL
H. Kennedy

## Into the East

One of the less-travelled-and-perhaps-more-charming-because-of-it parts of PEI is at the eastern end of the Island. Souris, named by French settlers for the plagues of mice that devoured the crops in the early eighteenth century, is near both the Basin Head Fisheries Museum and the Singing Sands Beach (where the atypically white sand squeaks because of its high silicone content). The area is also renowned for its fiddlers, particularly the Chaisson family, hosts of the annual Rollo Bay Fiddle Festival. Nearby is The Inn At Bay Fortune, once owned by playwright Elmer Harris (author of the critically acclaimed play *Johnny Belinda*), and more recently, by Colleen Dewhurst (the actress who played Marilla in the screen version of *Anne of Green Gables*).

# Nasturtium Salad with Goat Cheese and Poached Plums

### Goat Cheese Mixture

8 ounces fresh goat cheese

¼ cup chopped fresh mint, divided

2 tablespoons cracked black pepper, divided

1 teaspoon salt

### Poached Plums

1 cup sugar

½ cup port wine

½ cup water

12 ripe red plums

The charm of small-town life inspires chef Jeff McCourt to create innovative dishes in his country kitchen at The Inn At Bay Fortune. He uses local ingredients such as fruits, vegetables, and herbs from the inn's three-acre garden; wild chanterelles picked in the surrounding woods; Island lamb; and lobsters from the nearby wharf.

TO PREPARE GOAT CHEESE MIXTURE: In a food processor, combine goat cheese, 3 tablespoons mint, 1½ tablespoons pepper, and salt. Mix by pulsing until ingredients are well blended. Form mixture into a roll about 1½ inches in diameter. Mix remaining mint and pepper. Coat cheese roll with mint-pepper mixture, then cover and refrigerate. When ready to serve, cut cheese roll into ⅓-inch slices.

TO PREPARE POACHED PLUMS: In a medium saucepan, combine sugar, port, and water; bring to a gentle boil over medium-high heat. Reduce heat slightly and add four to six plums at a time, depending on size. (Do not crowd plums in pan.) Poach plums for 3 to 5 minutes or until fruit is soft and skin starts to break. Using a slotted spoon, transfer plums to a bowl to cool. Repeat until all plums are cooked. Peel cooked plums, then cover and refrigerate. Reserve poaching liquid.

TO PREPARE SPICY CRACKERS: In a food processor, combine semolina flour and salt. Start processor and pour half the water through feed tube in a steady stream. Add oil and Tabasco sauce. Add remaining water in a thin stream. Continue processing for 30 seconds or until dough forms a ball. Remove from processor and knead on a lightly floured surface for about 3 to 5 minutes or until dough is smooth and elastic. Cover and let rest for 30 minutes.

## Spicy Crackers

2 cups semolina flour

2 teaspoons salt

⅔ cup warm water, divided

4 teaspoons olive oil

Tabasco sauce to taste

Salt and coarsely ground black pepper

## Nasturtium Salad

½ cup cider vinegar

¼ cup olive oil

2 teaspoons honey

1 cup nasturtium petals

1 cup nasturtium leaves

Fresh mint, for garnish

4 nasturtium blossoms, for garnish

Preheat oven to 500°F. Roll out dough to form a 12x6-inch rectangle, then roll again until dough is about 1-inch thick. (The dough will be easier to handle if you let it relax for a few minutes each time you roll it.) Cut dough into sixteen rectangles (each about 1½ x 3 inches) and place on an ungreased baking sheet. Mist the dough with water, then sprinkle with salt and pepper. Bake at 500°F for 2 to 3 minutes or until crackers are lightly browned and crisp. Watch closely so the crackers don't burn. Remove from baking sheet and cool on a rack. Store in an airtight container.

TO PREPARE SALAD: In a mixing bowl, combine vinegar, oil, and honey; mix well. Add nasturtium petals and leaves; toss to coat with dressing.

To serve, place portions of salad on individual serving plates. Top each with three plums and four slices of goat cheese. Insert two crackers into each salad. Garnish with a drizzle of poaching syrup, fresh mint, and a nasturtium blossom.

*Yield: 4 servings*

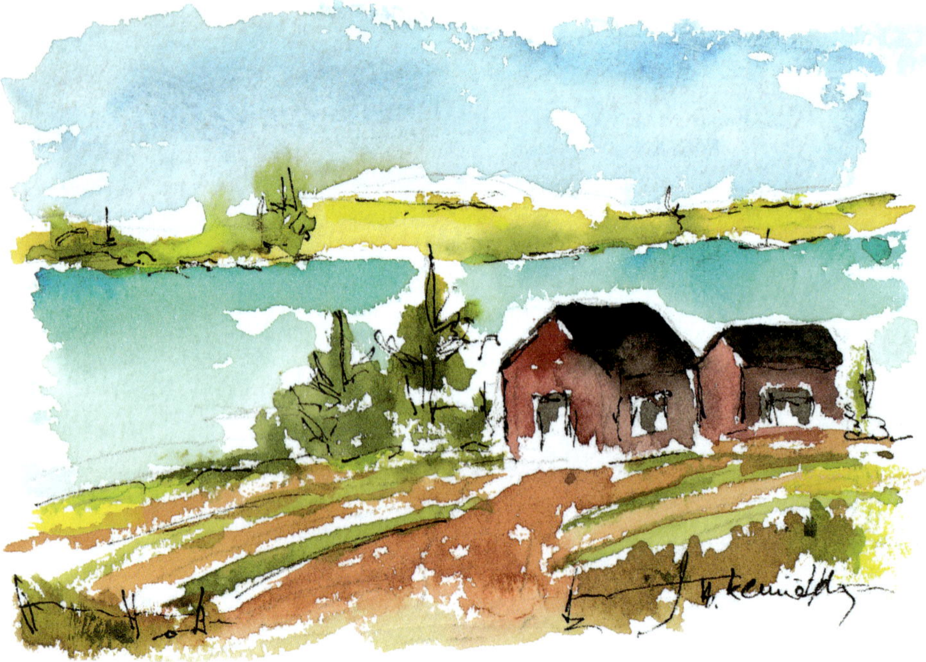

# *More Tastes of PEI*

Being so close to where food is grown and harvested is one of the attractions worth celebrating in Prince Edward Island. Nothing tastes quite so heavenly as a lobster that's gone straight from the ocean to the pot, or blueberries from the field to the bowl (with a dollop of fresh cream on top). Yes, you will find all those familiar restaurants that dot the rest of the planet, but you'll also find local favourites that take full advantage of the tasty treasures all around us. And where else will you find a roadside stand at the end of a lane, with a sign for "Potatoes" and a can of coins so you can make your own change?

# Catherine's Cranberry Loaf

Catherine McKinnon's rendition of the popular Canadian folk song "Farewell to Nova Scotia" earns as many plaudits as the food served at Catherine McKinnon's Spot O'Tea Restaurant in Stanley Bridge. Established by Catherine and her husband, writer/actor Don Harron, the restaurant is known for its codfish cakes, homemade beans, and delicious desserts. This is one of Catherine's personal recipes.

PREHEAT OVEN TO 325°F. Butter and flour a 9x5-inch loaf pan; set aside.

Grate rind from orange, then squeeze juice. Add enough boiling water to orange juice to make ¾ cup. In a mixing bowl, combine orange juice, orange rind, and butter; stir until butter melts. In another bowl, combine sugar and egg; beat well. Add sugar-egg mixture to orange mixture and mix well. Add cranberries and walnuts. Sift together flour, soda, and salt. Add dry ingredients to liquid mixture and mix well. Spoon batter into prepared pan and bake at 325°F for 1 hour. Serve warm.

*Yield: 1 loaf*

---

1 orange
Boiling water
2 tablespoons butter
1 cup sugar
1 egg
1 cup chopped cranberries
½ cup chopped walnuts
2 cups flour
½ teaspoon baking soda
½ teaspoon salt

# Tabouli

I n the late 1880s, the first Lebanese immigrants came to Prince Edward Island. They made their living as peddlers, travelling around the Island on foot or by horse and wagon to sell their wares. Over the years, they went on to establish some very successful businesses all over the Island, and today their descendants are an integral part of the community. Cedars Eatery in Charlottetown shares one of the great Lebanese contributions to Island life—their food—featuring such favourites as Falafel, Shawarma, Yabrak, and Tabouli.

¼ cup bulgur
3 cups finely chopped fresh parsley
3 ripe red tomatoes, finely diced
1 small onion, finely diced
¼ cup lemon juice
¼ cup olive oil
Salt and black pepper
Pita bread

PLACE BULGUR IN A LARGE BOWL and add enough cold water to cover; set aside to soak for 30 minutes. Drain well, squeezing out excess water. Combine bulgur with parsley, tomatoes, onion, lemon juice, and olive oil; mix well. Season with salt and pepper. Serve with pita bread.

*Yield: 6 servings*

# Kinkora Potato Soup

**4 tablespoons butter**
**6 green onions, finely chopped**
**3 small celery stalks, diced**
**1½ medium onions, chopped**
**6 PEI potatoes, thinly sliced**
**3 cups chicken stock**
**4 to 5 drops Worcestershire sauce**
**Dash of curry powder**
**Salt and pepper**
**¾ cup evaporated milk**
**¾ cup milk**

Prince Edward Islanders are fortunate to have in their midst some of the country's most state-of-the-art education and research facilities in the field of food production: the Agriculture Research Station, the Food Technology Centre, the Atlantic Veterinary College at the University of Prince Edward Island. And for years, the dynamic faculty at the Department of Home Economics (now Family and Nutritional Sciences) at UPEI have been educating students in the science—and art—of nutrition. Their version of a favourite soup features PEI potatoes.

MELT BUTTER in a heavy kettle. Add green onions, celery, and onions; sauté for about 5 minutes or until vegetables are tender but not brown. Add potatoes and chicken stock; cook for about 20 minutes or until potatoes are tender but not soft. Season with Worcestershire sauce, curry powder, salt, and pepper. Combine evaporated milk and milk; heat until hot but not boiling. Add hot milk to vegetable mixture and stir to mix. Serve steaming hot in mugs or crockery bowls.

*Yield: 6 servings*

# Selkirk Bannock

The Department of Family and Nutritional Sciences at UPEI shares another example of delicious Island comfort food—a hearty potato bread adapted from a traditional Scottish recipe.

PREHEAT OVEN TO 450ºF.

In a mixing bowl, combine flour, sugar, baking powder, and salt. Using a pastry blender, cut in shortening until mixture resembles coarse crumbs. Cut in mashed potatoes. Add just enough water to make a soft dough and mix quickly by hand. Turn out onto a lightly floured surface and knead gently for 8 to 10 minutes, dusting with additional flour as needed so the dough can be easily handled.

Form dough into a ten-inch circle and place on an ungreased cookie sheet, in a pie plate, or in a layer cake pan. Pat dough down to about ¾- to 1-inch thickness. Brush lightly with milk, if desired. Bake at 450º F for 17 to 20 minutes or until golden brown. Serve warm.

*Yield: 12 to 15 pieces*

---

2⅓ cups all-purpose flour

4 tablespoons sugar

2 teaspoons baking powder

1 teaspoon salt

4 tablespoons vegetable shortening

¾ cup mashed PEI potatoes

1 cup (approximately) water

Milk, to brush on dough (optional)

# Curried Seafood Chowder

A four-kilometre (two-and-a-half-mile) boardwalk runs along Charlottetown Harbour from Confederation Landing to Victoria Park. Near the boardwalk, the highly acclaimed Culinary Institute of Canada trains aspiring chefs who are leading their industry into the twenty-first century. The general public can enjoy a fine dining experience at the Institute—perhaps a meal featuring this tasty chowder.

IN A LARGE SOUP POT, combine celery, carrot, leek, onion, and oil. Cook over low heat, stirring occasionally, for 10 minutes or until vegetables lose their colour. Add peppercorns, thyme, tarragon, turmeric, curry powder, mustard seed, cayenne pepper, and honey. Cook for 5 minutes to release the flavours of the herbs and spices. Sprinkle flour into the mixture and stir to blend. Add chicken stock and potato; cook for 5 minutes. Add cream and cook, stirring occasionally, for 20 minutes or until soup begins to thicken. Season with salt and pepper. Add prawns, salmon, and scallops. Cook for about 15 to 20 minutes or just until seafood is done. Do not overcook seafood.

*Yield: 8 to 12 servings*

---

2 stalks celery, chopped

1 medium carrot, chopped

1 leek (white portion only), chopped

1 medium red onion, chopped

2 tablespoons vegetable oil

5 black peppercorns, crushed

3 sprigs fresh thyme

2 sprigs fresh tarragon

2 teaspoons turmeric

1½ tablespoons curry powder

1 tablespoon mustard seed

1 teaspoon cayenne pepper

2 tablespoons honey

2 tablespoons flour

1 litre (about 4½ cups) chicken stock

1 medium potato, chopped

1 litre (about 4½ cups) heavy cream

Salt and pepper

1 pound fresh prawns, peeled and deveined

1 pound fresh salmon, cut into 1-inch cubes

1 pound fresh scallops

# Boiled Lobster

The tradition of lobster suppers began in the 1960s as small communities around the Island celebrated the opening of lobster season along with the return of warm weather. The suppers were often a fundraising initiative for churches or other community organizations, with local fishermen and residents donating the food for the meal. Today there are several commercial lobster suppers in operation throughout the summer months—featuring lobster as the main course, of course! Menus vary from place to place, but most serve chowder and Island Blue mussels, hot or cold lobster, potato salad and coleslaw, fresh rolls and bread, and, for dessert, fresh berry pies and strawberry shortcake.

POUR SEAWATER INTO A LARGE COOKING POT until it is about three-fourths full. (If seawater is not available, add a handful of pickling salt to tap water.) Bring water to a rolling boil. Place medium-sized lobsters (about ¾ to 1 pound each) head first into the boiling water, one at a time. When the water returns to a boil, start timing and cook lobsters for 12 minutes. Do not overcook. Using tongs, remove lobsters from pot and place on a plate to drain.

Kitchen shears are useful when cracking the claws, and a long pointed skewer comes in handy for digging the meat out of the claws and legs. Most people prefer the lobster meat in the claws and the tail, although many enjoy the morsels of meat in the lobster body and the roe, which is found only in female lobsters. Try dipping the meat in melted garlic butter as you eat it. Whichever way you like it, be prepared to get messy!

# Seaweed Pie

The Seaweed Pie Café and Irish Moss Interpretive Centre is located in Miminegash near the Island's northwest tip, close to where Elephant Rock lost its "trunk" a few years ago from tidal erosion. Learn how Irish moss is harvested along the shore in the traditional way—using horses and scoops—and how the extracted carrageenan is used as a thickener in such foods as ice cream and custards. Take time to try a piece of delicious Seaweed Pie.

1¼ cups graham cracker crumbs
2 tablespoons packed brown sugar
½ teaspoon cinnamon
⅓ cup butter, melted
¾ cup (½ ounce) dried Irish moss
4 cups milk
2 strips orange rind
¼ cup plus 3 tablespoons granulated sugar, divided
1 tablespoon vanilla
2 cups strawberries
1 tablespoon lemon juice
½ cup whipping cream

GREASE A NINE-INCH PIE PLATE; set aside.

In a mixing bowl, combine graham cracker crumbs, brown sugar, and cinnamon. Add butter and mix with a fork until well blended. Press mixture evenly into bottom and sides of prepared pie plate. Refrigerate crust until ready to use.

Place moss in a small bowl, cover with cold water, and let soak for 15 minutes. Drain moss, then rinse well to remove any sand and drain again. In a medium saucepan, combine milk, orange rind, and ¼ cup granulated sugar; heat gently over medium heat. Add moss and simmer for 20 minutes, stirring often. Pour through a sieve to strain (do not press moss); discard moss and orange rind. Stir in vanilla. Pour mixture into pie crust. Refrigerate for at least 1 hour or until filling is completely set.

Place strawberries and lemon juice in blender container; purée until smooth. Stir in remaining 3 tablespoons granulated sugar; set aside. Beat whipping cream until soft peaks form. Pipe or spoon whipped cream onto chilled pie. Drizzle strawberry purée over slices of pie when serving.

Yield: 1 pie, 6 to 8 servings

NOTE: The traditional Seaweed Pie recipe calls for a layer of fresh fruit (such as strawberries, raspberries, or blueberries) on the graham cracker crust. Fresh fruit can also be used as a garnish in place of the strawberry purée.

This recipe may be made with unflavoured gelatin if dried Irish moss is not available. Reduce the amount of milk to 3½ cups, and combine milk, orange rind, and sugar in a saucepan. Sprinkle 2 envelopes unflavoured gelatin over milk mixture and let stand (do not heat) for 5 minutes. Then place pan over medium heat and heat gently until gelatin dissolves, about 5 minutes. Remove from heat and pour mixture into a large bowl. Stir in vanilla. Cover and refrigerate for about 1 hour or until mixture begins to thicken. Remove orange rind and pour filling into pie crust. Cover and refrigerate for about 1 hour or until filling is completely set.

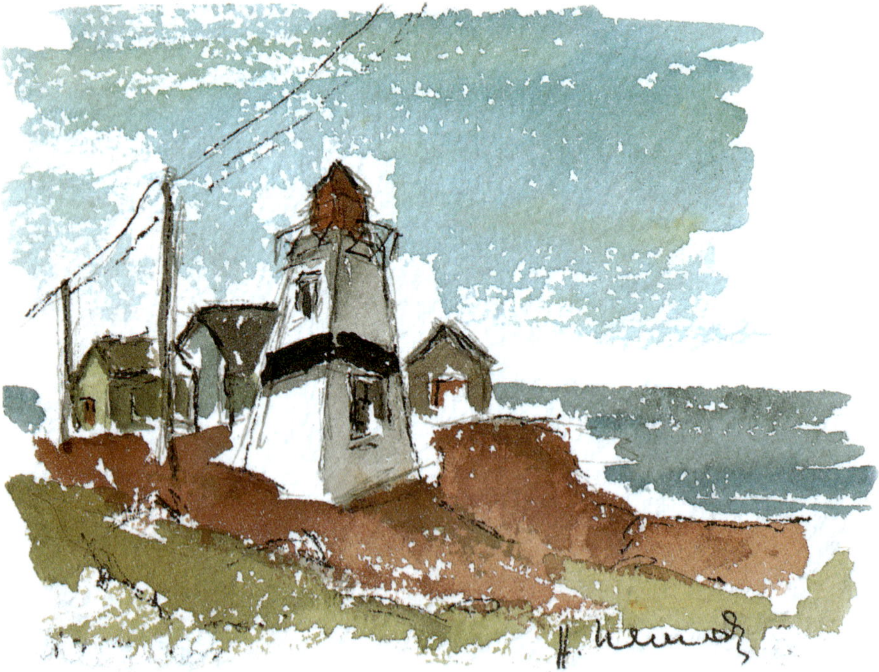

# Prince Edward Island Historical Timeline

| | |
|---|---|
| 8600 B.C. | First evidence of human habitation on the Island. |
| 1000 B.C. | The Island separates from the mainland. |
| 500–0 B.C. | First evidence of Mi'kmaq as the Island's aboriginal inhabitants. |
| 1000 | Vikings visit the area, calling it Vinland ("wine land" or "land of grapes"). |
| 1534 | Jacques Cartier visits the Island and names it Île-St-Jean (St. John's Island) because he arrives on St. John's Day. |
| 1720 | About two hundred French settlers come to Port LaJoye. Acadian families from the Bay of Fundy region arrive in Port LaJoye around the same time. |
| 1758 | Deportation of Acadians by the British. |
| 1763 | The Island officially comes under British rule. |
| 1764–5 | British captain Samuel Holland surveys the Island. |
| 1767 | The Island's land is distributed to British noblemen, merchants, and army officers in the Great Lottery. |
| 1769 | St. John's Island becomes a separate British colony with its own government. |
| 1773 | The Island Legislature is established. |
| 1799 | St. John's Island is renamed Prince Edward Island. |
| 1851 | Prince Edward Island achieves Responsible Government (self-rule). |
| 1864 | Charlottetown Conference is held in Province House to discuss Confederation of British North America's colonies. |
| 1867 | Canadian Confederation. The three colonies of Nova Scotia, New Brunswick, and Canada (now Quebec and Ontario) unite as the Dominion of Canada. |

| | |
|---|---|
| 1871 | Construction of the PEI Railway begins. |
| 1873 | Prince Edward Island joins Confederation. |
| 1874 | Lucy Maud Montgomery is born in Clifton (now New London). |
| 1908 | L. M. Montgomery's novel, *Anne of Green Gables*, is published. |
| 1917 | The Island gets its first car ferry, connecting Port Borden in Prince Edward Island with Cape Tormentine in New Brunswick. |
| 1922 | Women are given the franchise to vote. |
| 1964 | Opening of the Confederation Centre of the Arts, Canada's national memorial to the Fathers of Confederation. |
| 1969 | Founding of the University of Prince Edward Island. |
| 1989 | Trains stop running in Prince Edward Island. |
| 1993 | The Island elects Canada's first woman premier, the Hon. Catherine Callbeck. |
| 1997 | Confederation Bridge opens, connecting Borden-Carleton in Prince Edward Island with Cape Jourimain in New Brunswick. |
| 2000 | Confederation Trail is completed from one end of Prince Edward Island to the other. |

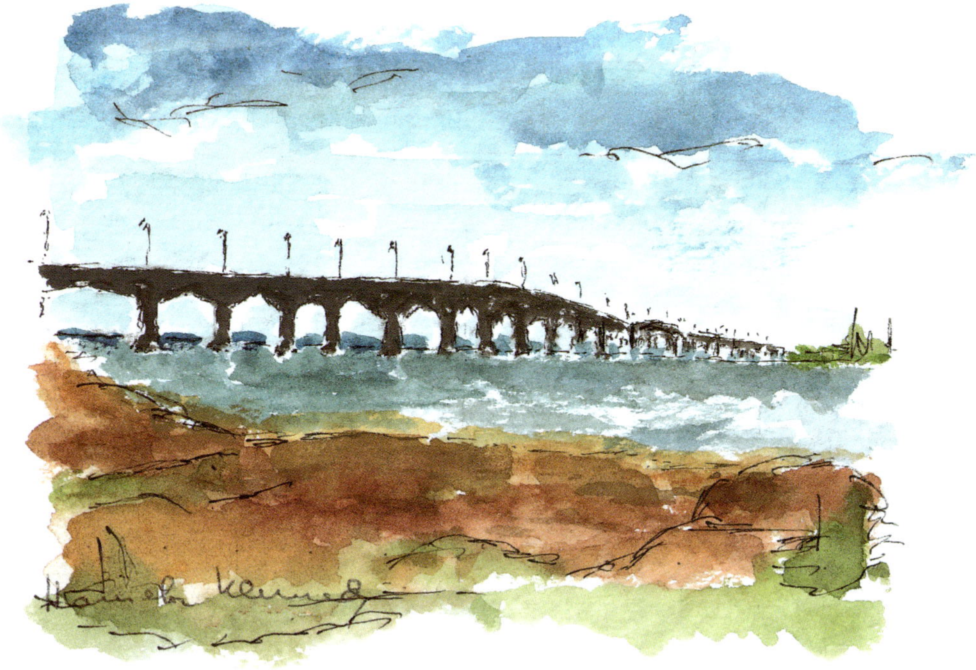

# Annual Festivals and Events

*February*   Charlottetown Winter Carnival

*May*   Spring Wine Festival, Charlottetown / Charlottetown Festival, Confederation Centre of the Arts *(end of May–mid-October)*

*June*   Bridgefest, Gateway Village, Borden-Carleton / Celtic Festival, College of Piping, Summerside *(June–August)* / Festival of Lights, Charlottetown, and Canada Day Celebrations *(end of June–July 1)* / Summerside Highland Gathering, College of Piping, Summerside / Tignish Irish Moss Festival *(end of June–July 1)* / Victoria Playhouse Festival, Victoria-by-the-Sea *(June–August)*

*July*   Charlottetown Race Week and Regatta / Crapaud Exhibition and PEI Tractor Pull *(end of July–early August)* / The Great Prince Edward Island Children's Festival, Beaconsfield, Charlottetown *(July–August)* / Indian River Festival, St. Mary's Church, Indian River *(July–August)* / Larry Gorman Folk Festival, Tyne Valley *(some years in August)* / Northumberland Fish Festival, Murray Harbour / PEI Potato Blossom Festival, O'Leary / Rendez-vous Rustico, South Rustico / Rollo Bay Fiddle Festival / St. Peters Wild Blueberry Festival, St. Peters Bay *(end of July–early August)* / Summerside Lobster Carnival / West Point Lighthouse Festival

*August*   Festival of the Fathers, Charlottetown *(end of August–early September)* / Kensington Harvest Festival / L'Exposition Agricole et le Festival Acadien, Abram-Village *(end of August–early September)* / Lucy Maud Montgomery Festival, Cavendish and area / Old Home Week and PEI Provincial Exhibition, Charlottetown / PEI Plowing Match and Agricultural Fair, Dundas / Tyne Valley Oyster Festival

*September*   International Shellfish Festival, Charlottetown / PEI Storytelling Festival, Island-wide / PEI Studio Tour, Island-wide / Trailfest, Confederation Trail, Island-wide

*December*   Wintertide Victorian Christmas Light Show, Charlottetown

*For more information, contact:*
*Tourism PEI*
*Phone 888.268.6677 or 902.368.7795*
*Web address www.peiplay.com*

# Index

## RECIPES

Boiled Lobster   59
Butterscotch Pie   18
Catherine's Cranberry Loaf   54
Coquilles St. Jacques   13
Creamy Carrot and Zucchini Soup   47
Curried Seafood Chowder   58
Fresh Atlantic Salmon en Papillote   26
Icebox Ginger Cookies   30
Kinkora Potato Soup   56
Maple-Roasted Pork Tenderloin with
    Fruit Confit   8
Nasturtium Salad with Goat Cheese and
    Poached Plums   50
New Moon Pudding   32
Nutmeg Scones   28
Oyster Stew   44
Pâté (Meat Pie)   15
Salmon Pie   34
Seaweed Pie   60
Seawinds Seafood Casserole   11
Selkirk Bannock   57
Shipwright's Oysters   24
Sticky Date Pudding with Toffee Sauce   42
Tabouli   55

## FEATURES

The Acadians   14
Charlottetown   7
Confederation Trail   43
Into the East   49
The Japanese Connection   31
The Land of *Anne*   27
Lighthouses   17
Made in PEI   33
Montague the Beautiful   46
Prince Edward Island National Park   40
Summerside   12
Tyne Valley   23
Victoria-by-the-Sea   10

*Prince Edward Island Memories* / 67